COME FOLLOW ME

THIS JOURNAL BELONGS TO

joyfulsaintspress.com

WANT FREE COLORING PAGES?

Go to https://bit.ly/36hG5GL to sign up & download

Copyright © 2022 by Caitlyn L Ashleigh
ALL RIGHTS RESERVED

2023 Come Follow Me Old Testament Schedule

- ❑ Dec 26 - Jan 1: Responsible For Our Learning
- ❑ Jan 2-8: Matthew 1; Luke 1
- ❑ Jan 9-15: Matthew 2; Luke 2
- ❑ Jan 16-22: John 1
- ❑ Jan 23-29: Matthew 3; Mark 1; Luke 3
- ❑ Jan 30 - Feb 5: Matthew 4; Luke 4-5
- ❑ Feb 6-12: John 2-4
- ❑ Feb 13-19: Matthew 5; Luke 6
- ❑ Feb 20-26: Matthew 6-7
- ❑ Feb 27 - Mar 5: Matthew 8; Mark 2-4; Luke 7
- ❑ Mar 6-12: Matthew 9-10; Mark 5; Luke 9
- ❑ Mar 13-19: Matthew 11-12; Luke 11
- ❑ Mar 20-26: Matthew 13; Luke 8; 13
- ❑ Mar 27 - Apr 2: Matthew 14; Mark 6; John 5-6
- ❑ Apr 3-9: Easter
- ❑ Apr 10-16: Matthew 15-17; Mark 7-9
- ❑ Apr 17-23: Matthew 18; Luke 10
- ❑ Apr 24-30: John 7-10
- ❑ May 1-7: Luke 12-17; John 11
- ❑ May 8-14: Matthew 19-20; Mark 10; Luke 18
- ❑ May 15-21: Matthew 21-23; Mark 11; Luke 19-20; John 12
- ❑ May 22-28: JS Matthew 1; Matthew 24-25; Mark 12-13; Luke 21
- ❑ May 29 - Jun 4: Matthew 26; Mark 14; John 13
- ❑ Jun 5-11: John 14-17
- ❑ June 12-18: Luke 22; John 18
- ❑ Jun 19-25: Matthew 27; Mark 15; Luke 23; John 19
- ❑ Jun 26 - Jul 2: Matthew 28; Mark 16; Luke 24; John 20-21
- ❑ Jul 3-9: Acts 1-5
- ❑ Jul 10-16: Acts 6-9
- ❑ Jul 17-23: Acts 10-15
- ❑ Jul 24-30: Acts 16-21
- ❑ Jul 31 - Aug 6: Acts 22-28
- ❑ Aug 7-13: Romans 1-6
- ❑ Aug 14-20: Romans 7-16
- ❑ Aug 21-27: 1 Corinthians 1-7
- ❑ Aug 28 – Sep 3: 1 Corinthians 8-13
- ❑ Sep 4-10: 1 Corinthians 14-16
- ❑ Sep 11-17: 2 Corinthians 1-7
- ❑ Sep 18-24: 2 Corinthians 8-13
- ❑ Sep 25 - Oct 1: Galatians
- ❑ Oct 2-8: Ephesians
- ❑ Oct 9-15: Philippians; Colossians
- ❑ Oct 16-22: 1 and 2 Thessalonians
- ❑ Oct 23-29: 1 and 2 Timothy; Titus; Philemon
- ❑ Oct 30 - Nov 5: Hebrews 1-6
- ❑ Nov 6-12: Hebrews 7-13
- ❑ Nov 13-19: James
- ❑ Nov 20-26: 1 and 2 Peter
- ❑ Nov 27 – Dec 3: 1-3 John; Jude
- ❑ Dec 4-10: Revelations 1-5
- ❑ Dec 11-17: Revelations 6-14
- ❑ Dec 18-24: Christmas
- ❑ Dec 25-31: Revelation 15-22

MY TESTIMONY

MY FAMILY CIRCLE

I AM SURROUNDED BY LOVE AND MY FAMILY. I AM NOT ALONE IN MY JOURNEY TO BECOME MORE LIKE JESUS CHRIST.

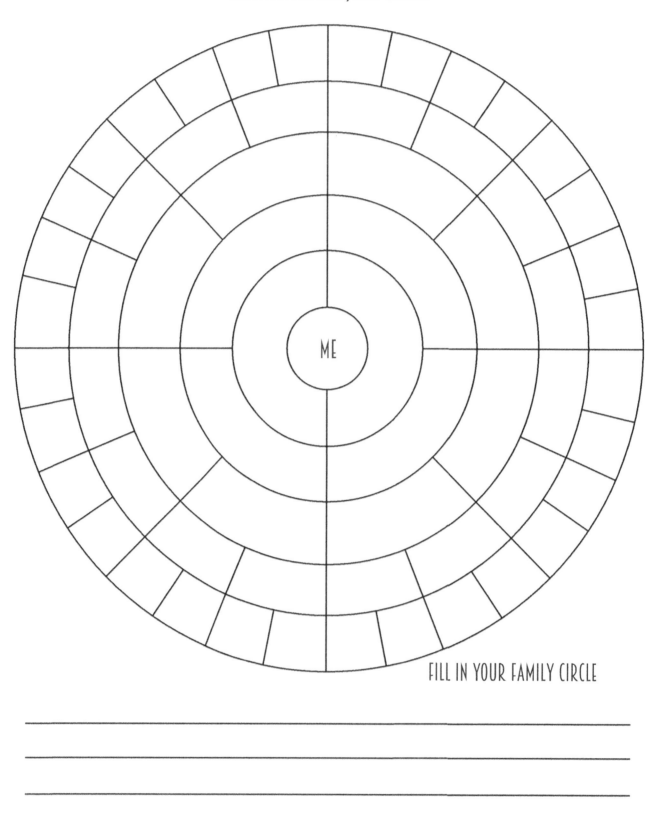

FILL IN YOUR FAMILY CIRCLE

MY GOALS THIS YEAR

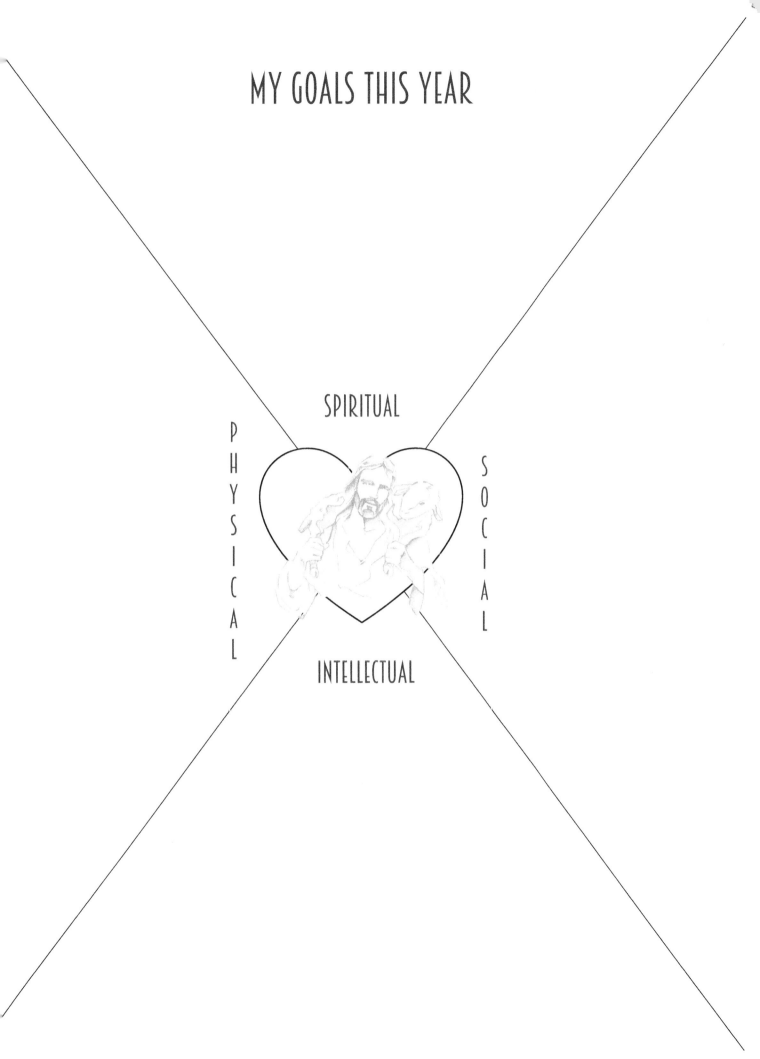

Dec 26 - Jan 1

Monday

John 1:38; Matthew 7:7 What do I seek this year? How does the Savior's promise to find what I seek inspire me for this upcoming year?

Tuesday

Matthew 19:16-22; Luke 18:18-23 What thoughts and emotions does the Savior's invitation to "Come, follow me" evoke?

Wednesday

Matthew 18:1-5; Luke 18:9-14 How can I use the Savior's teachings to humble myself and be taught by his words this year?

Thursday

John 13:1-15 How can Christ's words "I have given you an example, that ye should do as I have done unto you," guide my studies this year?

Responsible For Our Learning

Friday

John 7:17; James 1:5-6, 22; 2:17; 1 Nephi 10:17-19; D&C 18:18; 58:26-28
How can I take responsibility for my learning?

Saturday

Luke 11:9-13 John:5:39 What do I ask or search for this year?

Sunday Reflection

Spiritual Promptings

Goal for Next Week

Jan 2-8

Monday

Matthew 1:1-16 What do I learn from knowing Jesus's lineage?

Tuesday

Matthew 1: 17 – 25 What feelings do I have about the fact that Jesus was born to "save his people from their sins?"

Wednesday

Luke 1:1-20 What will help me believe in the Lord's promises even when they seem impossible?

Thursday

Luke 1:21-40 What great task or goal do I feel the Lord has given me?

Matthew 1; Luke 1

Friday — Luke 1:41-58 How does my soul magnify the Lord and my spirit rejoice in my Savior?

Saturday — Luke 1:59-80 How do I offer the light of Christ to those that sit in darkness?

Sunday Reflection

Spiritual Promptings

Goal for Next Week

Jan 9-15

Monday — Matthew 2:1-12 How do I worship the Lord?

Tuesday — Matthew 2:13-23 What promptings has the Lord given me to bless or save me?

Wednesday — Luke 2:1-12 What about Jesus's lowly birth helps me see that the Lord loves all of us?

Thursday — Luke 2:13-24 What about the Savior's birth fills me with wonder?

Matthew 2; Luke 2

Friday — Luke 2:25-39 What would it feel like to see salvation and know that the Savior had entered the world?

Saturday — Luke 2:40-52 Is it important to me to be about Heavenly Father's business?

Sunday Reflection

Spiritual Promptings

Goal for Next Week

Jan 16-22

Monday — John 1:1-5 What comfort do I feel that Jesus was with Heavenly Father from the beginning?

Tuesday — John 1:6-14 How is Christ a light in my life?

Wednesday — John 1:15-23 How can I be a "voice crying in the wilderness" declaring Christ's gospel this week?

Thursday — John 1:24-34 What inspires me about John's bold declaration that Jesus is the son of God?

John 1

Friday — John 1:35-42 What have I done this week to accept Christ's offer, "Come follow me?"

Saturday — John 1:43-51 Do I truly feel that Jesus knows me? Why?

Sunday Reflection

Spiritual Promptings

Goal for Next Week

Jan 23-29

Monday — Matthew 3:1-17 How does John's example of boldly preparing the world for Christ inspire me to do the same?

Tuesday — Mark 1:1-18 How does Jesus's baptism offer an example I can follow?

Wednesday — Mark 1:19-28 How does the Holy Ghost help me feel close to God?

Thursday — Mark 1:29-45 Does Christ's passion for others inspired me or give me a desire to help others?

Matthew 3; Mark 1; Luke 3

Friday

Luke 3:1-22 Did I feel Heavenly Father's love when I was baptized?

Saturday

Luke 3:23-38 How does knowing my family lineage give me comfort? Why is understanding Jesus's lineage important?

Sunday Reflection

Spiritual Promptings

Goal for Next Week

Jan 30 - Feb 5

Monday
Matthew 4: 1-12 Has there been a time when I felt tired or stressed? Did I feel more tempted during these times? What helped?

Tuesday
Matthew 4:13-25 What helps me recognize the light of Christ so that I may follow?

Wednesday
Luke 4:1-22 If Christ was called to help the poor and brokenhearted, what can I do this week to follow his example?

Thursday
Luke 4: 23-44 Would witnessing a miracle help me believe in Christ's power or is there something else?

Matthew 4; Luke 4-5

Friday

Luke 5:1-17 Christ withdrew into the wilderness to reconnect with Heavenly Father. Where do I connect best?

Saturday

Luke 5:18-39 When has my deep faith in Christ manifested a miracle or helped me feel forgiveness after I repented?

Sunday Reflection

Spiritual Promptings

Goal for Next Week

Feb 6-12

Monday — John 2 What about Christ turning water into wine was different than His other miracles? Why did it help the disciples believe?

Tuesday — John 3:1-17 How has my study of Christ's life and example saved me?

Wednesday — John 3:18-36 When has God's love and light given me courage or built my testimony?

Thursday — John 4:1-15 How can I gain perspective over my temporal needs so that I can focus on the "spiritual water?"

John 2-4

Friday — John 4:16-30 Am I a true worshiper of Christ and Heavenly Father?

Saturday — John 4:31-54 What work does the Lord call me to do? What can I do today?

Sunday Reflection

Spiritual Promptings

Goal for Next Week

Feb 13-19

Monday — Matthew 5:1-16 What traits do I feel I am blessed with?

Tuesday — Matthew 5:17-32 What traits or characteristics do I need to let go of or repent of?

Wednesday — Matthew 5:33-48 Has it ever been hard for me to love my enemies?

Thursday — Luke 6: 1-19 What would Christ see if He looked into my heart? What can I change today?

Matthew 5; Luke 6

Friday — Luke 6:20-34 Who can I pray for today that I might not normally think to pray for?

Saturday — Luke 6: 35-44 What can I work on to be more Christ like and see the good rather than imperfection?

Sunday Reflection

Spiritual Promptings

Goal for Next Week

Feb 20-26

Monday

Matthew 6:1-9 How can I change so that I do good and pray with true, Christ-like purpose rather than worry about the opinion of others?

Tuesday

Matthew 6:10-18   Have my prayers become repetitious? What can I do to improve?

Wednesday

Matthew 6:19-34 How can knowing that life on earth is but a moment but Christ's light is forever guide my actions?

Thursday

Matthew 7:1-8 What do I need to seek or know so that I can progress spiritually?

Matthew 6-7

Friday

Matthew 7:9-20 How can I improve my ability to find those that bring forth good actions?

Saturday

Matthew 7:21-29 When has my foundation, built upon Christ, saved me from the storm?

Sunday Reflection

Spiritual Promptings

Goal for Next Week

Feb 27 - Mar 5

Monday — Matthew 8 How can the scriptures or Christ's presence through the Holy Ghost calm the storms of my life?

Tuesday — Mark 2 What can I do to see into people's hearts like Christ did?

Wednesday — Mark 3 What good can I do on the upcoming Sabbath day?

Thursday — Mark 4 How is my own mustard seed grain? Am I feeding my testimony daily?

Matthew 8; Mark 2-4; Luke 7

Friday

Luke 7:1-23 What about the centurion's servant's healing interests me?

Saturday

Luke 7:24-50 How does forgiveness of my sins feel?

Sunday Reflection

Spiritual Promptings

Goal for Next Week

Mar 6 - 12

Monday — Matthew 9 What small miracles or everyday things strengthen my faith?

Tuesday — Matthew 10:1-20 Do I feel courage or comfort knowing the Lord will provide me the words to declare my testimony?

Wednesday — Matthew 10:21-42 What crosses must I shoulder to follow Christ?

Thursday — Mark 5 When do I need to remind myself to "be not afraid, only believe?"

Matthew 9-10; Mark 5; Luke 9

Friday

Luke 9:1-28 Christ fed the 5000 but how does His words feed my soul?

Saturday

Luke 9:29-62 When have I made excuses to do something first and then I can follow the Lord?

Sunday Reflection

Spiritual Promptings

Goal for Next Week

Mar 13 - 19

Monday — Matthew 11:1-15 John prepared the way for Jesus. How am I preparing the way for Christ's 2nd coming?

Tuesday — Matthew 11:16-30 When has leaning on Christ's strength made my burdens light?

Wednesday — Matthew 12:1-21 How can I focus on mercy and love on the Sabbath instead of sacrifice?

Thursday — Matthew 12:22-50 What words have I spoken that I might still need to repent of?

Matthew 11-12; Luke 11

Friday — Luke 11:1-26 How does the Holy Ghost speak to me when answering my prayers or questions?

Saturday — Luke 11:27-54 How can I make sure my inner soul is clean, not just my outer appearance?

Sunday Reflection

Spiritual Promptings

Goal for Next Week

Mar 20-26

Monday — Matthew 13:1-30 Have I ever sown tares into my own life? What helped me be free?

Tuesday — Matthew 13:31-58 What piece of the gospel is my "pearl of great price?"

Wednesday — Luke 8: 1-25 What helps me to establish "roots" in the gospel?

Thursday — Luke 8:26-56 What patterns of faith do I see in reading about Jesus's miracles? How can I improve my faith?

Matthew 13; Luke 8; 13

Friday — Luke 13:1-17 What can I cut out of my life?

Saturday — Luke 13:18-35 Why is it important to be prepared and strive to enter through the narrow gate?

Sunday Reflection

Spiritual Promptings

Goal for Next Week

Mar 27 - Apr 2

Monday

Matthew 14 Am I careful in the promises and oaths I make?

Tuesday

Mark 6:1-29 Would I have the faith to take nothing for my journey or mission?

Wednesday

Mark 6:30-56 When have I felt like a sheep without a shepherd? What helps to keep me grounded?

Thursday

John 5 How do I feel about the idea that the gospel is shared with those that are dead?

Matthew 14; Mark 6; John 5-6

Friday — John 6:1-40 If I saw Jesus walking on water, would I feel fear or awe?

Saturday — John 6:41-71 Does taking the sacrament each week fulfill or help me?

Sunday Reflection

Spiritual Promptings

Goal for Next Week

My Testimony of this Conference

Notes

Apr 3-9

Monday — Matthew 21 The people honored Jesus when He entered Jerusalem. Do I honor Jesus?

Tuesday — Matthew 22-23 How can I follow Christ's teachings to love others this week?

Wednesday — Matthew 24-25 What is the most important thing I can do this week to prepare myself and others for the 2nd coming?

Thursday — Matthew 26 What speaks to my soul about Christ's prayers and suffering at Gethsemane?

Easter

Friday — Matthew 27 Instead of sorrow, how can Christ's crucifixion soften my heart and help me to do good?

Saturday — Matthew 28:1-10 As Easter approaches, how can reflecting on Christ's resurrection inspire me to live the gospel?

Sunday Reflection

Spiritual Promptings

Goal for Next Week

Apr 10-16

Monday

Matthew 15 What teaching of the gospel do I pay lip service to? How can I soften my heart to do better?

Tuesday

Matthew 16 How has the priesthood and sealing power to bind on earth and heaven blessed me?

Wednesday

Matthew 17 How can I grow my faith so that it is unshakeable to the point I believe that nothing is impossible for God?

Thursday

Mark 7 What one thing can I do today to strengthen my heart and mind to resist temptation?

Matthew 15-17; Mark 7-9

Friday — Mark 8 How can Christ's miracle of feeding the 400 help me to know that Heavenly Father will multiply my righteous efforts?

Saturday — Mark 9 When have I cried out ,"Lord help thou mine unbelief?" When has fasting and prayer helped?

Sunday Reflection

Spiritual Promptings

Goal for Next Week

Apr 17-23

Monday — Matthew 18:1-6 Deeply ponder. How can I humble myself as a little child?

Tuesday — Matthew 18:7-20 What can I do to try to not be offended?

Wednesday — Matthew 18:21-35 Who do I need to forgive? Do I need to repent and forgive myself?

Thursday — Luke 10:1-16 Jesus sent his 70 out to preach and heal. What charge has the prophet given me?

Matthew 18; Luke 10

Friday

Luke 10:17-25 What state of mind or in what place do I need to be in to feel the will of the Lord?

Saturday

Luke 10:26-42 Who is my neighbor? Do I have compassion for all even if they are different?

Sunday Reflection

Spiritual Promptings

Goal for Next Week

Apr 24-30

Monday — John 7:1-31 By doing service and the will of the Lord, do I better understand the gospel?

Tuesday — John 7:32-53 How is the Holy Ghost a gift in my life? Does he bear witness of the truth?

Wednesday — John 8:1-32 What stones do I cast? How can I remember my own imperfect nature before judging others?

Thursday — John 8:33-59 How can I honor Heavenly Father in my words and deeds?

John 7-10

Friday — John 9 How does my study of the gospel open my spiritual eyes?

Saturday — John 10 What actions help me better hear the Lord and follow Him?

Sunday Reflection

Spiritual Promptings

Goal for Next Week

May 1-7

Monday — Luke 12 If Heavenly Father values every hair on His children's heads, then how should I treat others?

Tuesday — Luke 13 When have my own sins caused me to weep? Does repentance fill me with joy?

Wednesday — Luke 14 How does Christ's love and example help me follow Him even with my trials?

Thursday — Luke 15-16 Do I forgive with a full heart and welcome those that wrong me with joy?

Luke 12-17; John 11

Friday — Luke 17 Am I like the tenth leper? Do I recognize the miracles, even small ones, the Lord blesses me with?

Saturday — John 11 How has following the principles of the gospel shone light on my path and helped me not to stumble?

Sunday Reflection

Spiritual Promptings

Goal for Next Week

May 8-14

Monday

Matthew 19 What treasures of the world do I willing give up to follow the Lord? Can I give up one more small thing this week?

Tuesday

Matthew 20 How can I avoid jealously and instead focus on the gifts the Lord gives me instead of others?

Wednesday

Mark 10:1-27 How strong are my relationships?

Thursday

Mark 10:28-52 What can I do this week to be a servant of all?

Matthew 19-20; Mark 10; Luke 18

Friday

Luke 18:1-17 How might I need to humble myself so that I can hear Him?

Saturday

Luke 18:18-43 How can I be more like the blind man who continued to cry out to the Lord even if the world tries to quiet me?

Sunday Reflection

Spiritual Promptings

Goal for Next Week

May 15-21

Monday — Matthew 21 Am I more like the first son who refused and repented or the second who agreed and went not?

Tuesday — Matthew 22 When has the Lord called me? Did I accept? What fears/challenges did I overcome?

Wednesday — Matthew 23 Am I too worried about the little things rather than concerning myself with the weightier laws?

Thursday — Mark 11 Is Christ my king? How do I rejoice or worship Him daily?

Matthew 21-23; Mark 11; Luke 19-20; John 12

Friday — Luke 19-20 How can I follow Christ yet live in this imperfect world?

Saturday — John 12 When has my hardened heart blinded me to truth and righteousness?

Sunday Reflection

Spiritual Promptings

Goal for Next Week

May 22-28

Monday

Joseph Smith-Matthew 1 How can I treasureth up Christ's words and draw comfort and faith from Him?

Tuesday

Matthew 24 What thing or things should I stop doing so that I may spend more time preparing for the Lord's coming?

Wednesday

Matthew 25 What talents and gifts have I been given? How am I developing those talents?

Thursday

Mark 12 When have I cast in my two mites and given my all for the Lord's cause?

JS Matthew; Matthew 24-25; Mark 12-13; Luke 21

Friday — Mark 13 What fills me with peace or comfort so that I may endure to the end?

Saturday — Luke 21 How does my gospel foundation provide me refuge in times of tribulation?

Sunday Reflection

Spiritual Promptings

Goal for Next Week

May 29 - Jun 4

Monday — Matthew 26:1-35 How can I honor the Lord even if the world might think my efforts are a waste?

Tuesday — Matthew 26:36-75 Does Christ's words "not as I will, but as thou wilt" inspire me to endue through my trials?

Wednesday — Mark 14:1-31 How can I be more in tune with Christ and the Holy Ghost when I take the sacrament?

Thursday — Mark 14:32-72 How has prayer and vigilance helped me avoid temptation?

Matthew 26; Mark 14; John 13

Friday

John 13:1-17 The devil put thoughts of betrayal in Juda's heart. What weakness can I strengthen to sure up my heart against Satan?

Saturday

John 13:18-38 What thoughts of service does Christ's words to "love one another" inspire?

Sunday Reflection

Spiritual Promptings

Goal for Next Week

Jun 5-11

Monday — John 14:1-14 How does Christ's declaration "I am the way, the truth, and the life," offer a solid foundation for my actions?

Tuesday — John 14:15-31 How does Christ's and Heavenly Father's promise of love reaffirm my desire to follow the commandments?

Wednesday — John 15:1-15 When has keeping the commandments filled me with joy?

Thursday — John 15:16-27 How can I bear witness this week of Jesus Christ and His gospel?

John 14-17

Friday — 1 Samuel 2 When have I recently prayed and "rejoiceth in the Lord?"

Saturday — 1 Samuel 3 How can I avoid letting none of the Lord's "words fall to the ground?"

Sunday Reflection

Spiritual Promptings

Goal for Next Week

June 12-18

Monday — Luke 22:1-20 What does taking the bread and water of the sacrament each week mean to me?

Tuesday — Luke 22:21-39 Is greatness or stature important to me? Why?

Wednesday — Luke 22:40-53 Even though Jesus had been betrayed, He healed the man who captured Him. Do I have that sort of compassion?

Thursday — Luke 22:54-71 Christ suffered and died for me. What can help me remember that so I do not deny Him like Peter?

Luke 22; John 18

Friday

John 18:1-23 Jesus knew His fate and faced it with courage. When has the Lord given me courage to choose the right?

Saturday

John 18:24-40 Can I find purpose for my own life through Christ's words, to this end I was born that I should bear witness unto the truth?

Sunday Reflection

Spiritual Promptings

Goal for Next Week

Jun 19-25

Monday — Matthew 27:1-38 Jesus suffered with grace and calm because He loved me. How can I show my love for the Savior this week?

Tuesday — Matthew 27:39-66 In the moments before Christ's death, He felt forsaken and alone. How has the companionship of the Holy Ghost comforted me?

Wednesday — Mark 15 Christ endured mocking and pain. How can His example help me stay strong in my faith even if the world mocks me?

Thursday — Mark 23:1-26 Have I ever done no wrong yet the wickedness of the world cries out to punish me?

Matthew 27; Mark 15; Luke 23; John 19

Friday — Mark 23:27-56 Jesus openly forgave his tormentors. Can I show love by doing the same?

Saturday — John 19 Pilate knew crucifying Jesus was wrong, but he let it happen. Have I let wrong things happen just to keep the peace?

Sunday Reflection

Spiritual Promptings

Goal for Next Week

Jun 26 - Jul 2

Monday

Matthew 28 The woman felt both "fear and great joy" because of Christ's resurrection. What would I have felt in that moment?

Tuesday

Mark 16 How has Jesus's resurrection affected my mindset, life, and beliefs?

Wednesday

Luke 24:1-29 His disciples walked with Him and did not recognize Him. When has my lack of faith blinded me from the truth?

Thursday

Luke 24:30-53 The disciples stood as witnesses. How can I stand as a witness of the gospel?

Matthew 28; Mark 16; Luke 24; John 20-21

Friday

John 20 Does Jesus's promise that "blessed are they that have not seen and yet have believed" strengthened my faith?

Saturday

John 21 How can I feed the Lord's sheep this upcoming week?

Sunday Reflection

Spiritual Promptings

Goal for Next Week

Jul 3-9

Monday — Acts 1 The Lord entrusted the building up of His church to the apostles with the guidance of the Holy Ghost. How can this help me trust the Holy Ghost?

Tuesday — Acts 2 What can I do to work toward having "all things in common" with others and creating real harmony?

Wednesday — Acts 3 Peter proclaimed it was not his power that healed the lame man. Do I acknowledge Heavenly Father's power in my daily life?

Thursday — Acts 4 Have I felt so in tune with the Holy Ghost that I felt "of one heart and of one soul?"

Acts 1-5

Friday

Acts 5:1-16 The Lord knows my heart. Is there any untruth or concern I need to take to the Lord?

Saturday

Acts 5:17-42 Do I think that I have or could have the faith necessary to rejoice that I suffered in Christ's name?

Sunday Reflection

Spiritual Promptings

Goal for Next Week

Jul 10-16

Monday — Acts 6 Have I trusted in the Holy Ghost to help me speak with truth, wisdom, and the spirit?

Tuesday — Acts 7:1-36 When have I struggled like Joseph or Moses and sought out the Lord and Holy Ghost to help me?

Wednesday — Acts 7:37-60 Have I resisted the influence of the Holy Ghost?

Thursday — Acts 8 Simon's offer of money for the Holy Ghost wasn't in the right spirit. Have I ever sought for the Holy Ghost's influence while not in the right frame of mind?

Acts 6-9

Friday — Acts 9:1-22 What about Saul's conversion inspires me?

Saturday — Acts 9:23-43 Am I someone who is known for their good works?

Sunday Reflection

Spiritual Promptings

Goal for Next Week

Jul 17-23

Monday — Acts 10 How can remembering <u>all</u> are children of God help me treat all with love?

Tuesday — Acts 11 How can listening for the Holy Ghost open my heart and bless others' lives?

Wednesday — Acts 12 Who might need my unceasing prayers this week?

Thursday — Acts 13 Even if my efforts to share the gospel are not successful, am I able to turn to the Lord to find joy and the will to try again?

Acts 10-15

Friday — Acts 14 What small thing can I do or have I done for someone to open a door of faith?

Saturday — Acts 15 What did I learn about how disagreements can be settled?

Sunday Reflection

Spiritual Promptings

Goal for Next Week

Jul 24-30

Monday — Acts 16 Paul and Silas prayed and sang when jailed. What lessons can I learn from their actions?

Tuesday — Acts 17 What things do I ignorantly worship?

Wednesday — Acts 18 How can the Lord's words to Paul, "be not afraid, but speak" give me courage?

Thursday — Acts 19 What filled my heart when I received the Holy Ghost or how will it feel?

Acts 16-21

Friday — Acts 20 Does giving fill me with more joy than receiving? Why?

Saturday — Acts 21 Do I feel enough at peace with myself to say, "the will of the Lord be done?"

Sunday Reflection

Spiritual Promptings

Goal for Next Week

Jul 31 - Aug 6

Monday

Acts 22 What opportunities do I have to share my testimony and personal conversion to the gospel?

Tuesday

Acts 23 When have I felt the Lord's support and council to "be of good cheer?"

Wednesday

Acts 24 -25 Is my "conscience void of offense toward God?"

Thursday

Act 26 Do I bear witness of both the small and great things the Lord has blessed me with?

Acts 22-28

Friday — Acts 27 How might I have felt if Paul told me to fear not, I would not lose my life but instead be shipwrecked?

Saturday — Acts 28 Has there been a time when my heart hardened and I was slow to hear Him?

Sunday Reflection

Spiritual Promptings

Goal for Next Week

Aug 7-13

Monday — Romans 1 Who or what do I mention always in my prayers?

Tuesday — Romans 2 What judgement(s) do I fear?

Wednesday — Romans 3 Though "all have sinned," how can my faith in Christ make up for my shortcomings?

Thursday — Romans 4 What outward or inward signs do I have to demonstrate my faith in Christ?

Romans 1-6

Friday — Romans 5 What feelings come to mind when I read "by the obedience of one shall many be made righteous?"

Saturday — Romans 6 Do I feel "free from sin" when I repent?

Sunday Reflection

Spiritual Promptings

Goal for Next Week

Aug 14-20

Monday — Romans 7-8 When have I seen the principle that all things work together for good?

Tuesday — Romans 9-10 Are my "feet beautiful" because I strive to preach the gospel?

Wednesday — Romans 11 What might I need to give up to "continue in His goodness?"

Thursday — Romans 12-13 Do I think too highly of myself in any area? How can I be more humble?

Romans 7-16

Friday — Romans 14-15 How can I avoid contention and judgement of others?

Saturday — Romans 16 What can I do or look for to be wise unto that which is good?

Sunday Reflection

Spiritual Promptings

Goal for Next Week

Aug 21-27

Monday — 1 Corinthians 1 How are my efforts to fellowship and be kind to others going?

Tuesday — 1 Corinthians 2 What "deep things of God" has the Holy Ghost manifested unto me?

Wednesday — 1 Corinthians 3 What are my foundations? Is Christ the most important one?

Thursday — 1 Corinthians 4 Would I be accounted as a minister of Christ?

1 Corinthians 1-7

Friday

1 Corinthians 5-6 Do I treat my body as a temple, a place where the Holy Ghost can reside?

Saturday

1 Corinthians 7 Am I faithful and loving in all my relationships?

Sunday Reflection

Spiritual Promptings

Goal for Next Week

Aug 28 – Sep 3

Monday — 1 Corinthians 8 What idols of the worlds distract me from fulfilling Heavenly Father's purpose for me?

Tuesday — 1 Corinthians 9 What can help me choose daily to be a servant to all?

Wednesday — 1 Corinthians 10 How does knowing that God will help me escape any temptation aid me in enduring to the end?

Thursday — 1 Corinthians 11 Do I take the sacrament each week with a pure heart and take the opportunity to repent?

1 Corinthians 8-13

Friday — 1 Corinthians 12 What are my spiritual gifts? How do I or can I help others with these gifts?

Saturday — 1 Corinthians 13 What is my self assessment on my faith, hope, and charity? What do I want to adjust?

Sunday Reflection

Spiritual Promptings

Goal for Next Week

Sep 4-10

Monday — 1 Corinthians 14:1-20 What talent, skill, or spiritual gift do I want? How do I want to use it?

Tuesday — 1 Corinthians 14:21-40 How do I handle confusing ideas or doctrine? Do I seek the Lord's council?

Wednesday — 1 Corinthians 15:1-22 If I did not believe in the resurrection of Christ, how would my life be different?

Thursday — 1 Corinthians 15:23-39 Would the mantra "eat and drink, for tomorrow we die" change my current path? How?

1 Corinthians 14-16

Friday — 1 Corinthians 15:40-58 What spiritual body do I want? How do I labor daily to be worthy of it?

Saturday — 1 Corinthians 16 How do I stand fast in faith?

Sunday Reflection

Spiritual Promptings

Goal for Next Week

Sep 11-17

Monday

2 Corinthians 1 Have I witnessed the power of a group praying for someone?

Tuesday

2 Corinthians 2 How can I be more understanding and forgiving of church leaders and members since we all walk imperfectly?

Wednesday

2 Corinthians 3 When has the spirit of the Lord opened my eyes and offered freedom?

Thursday

2 Corinthians 4 How do Paul's words "our light affliction, which is but a moment" give me eternal perspective?

2 Corinthians 1-7

Friday — 2 Corinthians 5 What daily habits do I have or can build to help me "walk by faith, not by sight?"

Saturday — 2 Corinthians 6-7 Which traits mentioned by Paul might I need to improve to be a minister of God?

Sunday Reflection

Spiritual Promptings

Goal for Next Week

Sep 18-24

Monday — 2 Corinthians 8 What do I do with my abundance (money, time, or talents)?

Tuesday — 2 Corinthians 9 Do I give with cheer or give out of a sense of responsibility? When am I most cheerful giving?

Wednesday — 2 Corinthians 10 What can I do to look beyond outward appearances and see others as children of God?

Thursday — 2 Corinthians 11 How is the gospel simple? How can I focus on the simple acts of discipleship?

2 Corinthians 8-13

Friday

2 Corinthians 12 What weakness of mine, with Christ's help, can be strengthened?

Saturday

2 Corinthians 13 Can I examine myself and see if I "be in the faith?" What would that look like to me?

Sunday Reflection

Spiritual Promptings

Goal for Next Week

Sep 25 - Oct 1

Monday

Galatians 1 Do other's words or deeds easily sway me from the gospel?

Tuesday

Galatians 2 Do my actions demonstrate that the light of Christ liveth in me?

Wednesday

Galatians 3 What promises do I receive as a seed of Abraham through baptism?

Thursday

Galatians 4 How are the lives of an heir and servant different? How does being an heir of God make my life different?

Galatians

Friday — Galatians 5 Am I walking in the spirit? Have I noticed any results from spiritual living?

Saturday — Galatians 6 Have I ever been weary of doing well? Did I push past my weariness?

Sunday Reflection

Spiritual Promptings

Goal for Next Week

Oct 2-8

Monday — Ephesians 1 How do I feel about living in the depensation of the fullness of times?

Tuesday — Ephesians 2 Is Christ the cornerstone of my life? Why or why not?

Wednesday — Ephesians 3 Are there times I feel lost or adrift? How can I root myself in faith and love?

Thursday — Ephesians 4 Is there any anger or bitterness I need to put away?

Ephesians

Friday — Ephesians 5 Do I walk as a child of light? Is something keeping the light out?

Saturday — Ephesians 6 What part of my armor of God is the strongest? The weakest?

Sunday Reflection

Spiritual Promptings

Goal for Next Week

My Testimony of this Conference

Notes

Oct 9-15

Monday — Philippians 1 What does it feel like when I am standing fast with one spirit and one mind?

Tuesday — Philippians 2 Am I at peace with myself in this moment? Would I sacrifice to find joy?

Wednesday — Philippians 3-4 Do I seek what is true, honest, just, pure, lovely, things of good report, or virtuous?

Thursday — Colossians 1 Have I prayed for the knowledge of His will lately?

Philippians; Colossians

Friday — Colossians 2 Am I easily pulled away from things Christ would want me to do?

Saturday — Colossians 3-4 How can I be reminded daily to set my affections on the things above?

Sunday Reflection

Spiritual Promptings

Goal for Next Week

Oct 16-22

Monday — 1 Thessalonians 1-2 Do I feel joy in being a missionary?

Tuesday — 1 Thessalonians 3 Can I perfect that which is lacking in my faith?

Wednesday — 1 Thessalonians 4 What might I need to decrease so that I am able to increase my faith more and more?

Thursday — 1 Thessalonians 5 Paul encourages us to rejoice, pray, give thanks, and abstain from evil. Which of these can I improve?

1 and 2 Thessalonians

Friday

2 Thessalonians 1-2 What do I know about the Great Apostasy? Am I grateful for the Restoration?

Saturday

2 Thessalonians 3 Do I ever feel weary? What encourages me?

Sunday Reflection

Spiritual Promptings

Goal for Next Week

Oct 23-29

Monday — 1 Timothy 1-3 What true, constant, and unchangeable doctrines do I hold to?

Tuesday — 1 Timothy 4-6 Do I treat the elderly with love and care? How?

Wednesday — 2 Timothy 1-2 What good things do I hold unto that fill me with the Holy Ghost?

Thursday — 2 Timothy 3-4 Do I continually seek to learn more about Christ?

1 and 2 Timothy; Titus; Philemon

Friday — Titus 1-3 What habits can I put in place to help me do good works?

Saturday — Philemon 1 Can I let go of the past to accept and fully fellowship others?

Sunday Reflection

Spiritual Promptings

Goal for Next Week

Oct 30 - Nov 5

Monday
Hebrews 1 Do I love righteousness as Heavenly Father and Christ do? Do I demonstrate this trait?

Tuesday
Hebrews 2 How is Jesus Christ like a captain, someone who serves and guides?

Wednesday
Hebrews 3 Do I err in my heart? What can I do to change?

Thursday
Hebrews 4 Do I look to Jesus Christ when I am in trouble and in need of mercy and grace?

Hebrews 1-6

Friday — Hebrews 5 Instead of being a teacher of the gospel have I had need to be taught because I was dull of hearing?

Saturday — Hebrews 6 Is my goal to strive toward perfection?

Sunday Reflection

Spiritual Promptings

Goal for Next Week

Nov 6-12

Monday — Hebrews 7 What blessings have I received through the Melchizedek Priesthood?

Tuesday — Hebrews 8-9 Can I understand why the Jews might have felt lost and confused by having to give up their traditions to accept Christ?

Wednesday — Hebrews 10 Are the Lord's laws written on my heart? Has the Holy Ghost witnessed these truths to me?

Thursday — Hebrews 11 How do these stories of faith inspire me?

Hebrews 7-13

Friday — Hebrews 12 Why is chastening an act of love?

Saturday — Hebrews 13 Paul preaches many virtues such as brotherly love, marriage, and Christ's eternal nature. Which idea(s) capture my attention?

Sunday Reflection

Spiritual Promptings

Goal for Next Week

Nov 13-19

Monday

James 1:1-16 Do I ask for wisdom with unwavering faith? What answers have I received?

Tuesday

James 1:17-27 Am I a doer of the word? If not, what one small thing can I do today?

Wednesday

James 2 What thoughts, images, and ideas does the counsel "faith without works is dead" evoke?

Thursday

James 3 Is there any bitter envy or strife I need to purge from my heart? How would letting it go feel?

James

Friday — James 4 What might I need to do to resist the devil and draw nigh unto Heavenly Father?

Saturday — James 5 Gold, silver, and even the earth is temporary. How can this perspective encourage me to seek out heavenly treasures?

Sunday Reflection

Spiritual Promptings

Goal for Next Week

Nov 20-26

Monday — 1 Peter 1 What trial of faith have I faced?

Tuesday — 1 Peter 2 Have I encountered stumbling blocks when I am not living as righteous as I should?

Wednesday — 1 Peter 3 Am I always ready to give anyone the message of love and hope that the gospel offers?

Thursday — 1 Peter 4-5 Would I be excited to teach and be a missionary to those in the spirit world?

1 and 2 Peter

Friday — 2 Peter 1 Do I rely on and recognize the power the Holy Ghost can offer when studying my scriptures?

Saturday — 2 Peter 2-3 How can I make sure that the world's unbelief in the second coming and wickedness does not color my own view or actions?

Sunday Reflection

Spiritual Promptings

Goal for Next Week

Nov 27 – Dec 3

Monday — 1 John 1-2 How does it feel to have Jesus Christ as an advocate for me to Heavenly Father?

Tuesday — 1 John 3 Does my joy feel full of light? How does untruth or unrighteousness feel like darkness?

Wednesday — 1 John 4 What examples can I name that demonstrate that "love is of God?"

Thursday — 1 John 5 Why do I desire eternal life? What would I want to do in the eternities?

1-3 John; Jude

Friday — 2 John - 3 John When have I felt joy for someone who was found or experienced the light of Christ?

Saturday — Jude Do I contend for the faith? Do I advocate for Christ?

Sunday Reflection

Spiritual Promptings

Goal for Next Week

Dec 4-10

Monday — Revelations 1 Make a list of the things this chapter says about who Christ is and what he does for me.

Tuesday — Revelations 2:1-11 Is eating of the tree of life and being in Heavenly Father's presence a worthy goal? How can this goal remind me to repent?

Wednesday — Revelations 2:12-29 What can I learn from all the kingdoms who were given the gospel yet still rebelled?

Thursday — Revelations 3 Imagine the image of Christ standing at the door waiting on me. What feelings does it evoke?

Revelation 1-5

Friday — Revelations 4 What does it mean to worship the Lord? How do I worship?

Saturday — Revelations 5 Why is Christ depicted as a lamb? Why do I feel He was worthy to open the seals and redeem the world?

Sunday Reflection

Spiritual Promptings

Goal for Next Week

Dec 11-17

Monday — Revelations 6 What insights do I see studying the various seals and timeframes they represent?

Tuesday — Revelations 7-8 How can the imagery and depiction of Christ in these verses help calm any fears about the 2nd coming?

Wednesday — Revelations 9 What does the imagery in this chapter tell me about the last days?

Thursday — Revelations 10-11 John was invited to prophesize to many in the last days. What is my role during this time?

Revelation 6 -14

Friday — Revelations 12-13 How do I see Satan continuing to wage war on the earth today?

Saturday — Revelations 14 Do I see the Lord's love and patience in these verses and His continual desire to help people hear the gospel?

Sunday Reflection

Spiritual Promptings

Goal for Next Week

Dec 18-24

Monday

Matthew 1:18-25; 2:1-12 How does remembering the Savior's birth help me bring light into the lives of others this season?

Tuesday

Luke 1:26-38; 2:1-20 "For unto you is born this day…Christ the Lord." Can I take a moment, in this busy season, to appreciate that truth?

Wednesday

Jesus Christ Section His Birth in the Gospel Library   What insights about the Savior and His birth did I gain?

Thursday

1 Corinthians 15:21-26 Colossians 1:12-22 1 Peter 2:21-25 How can I show Christ that I appreciate His mission to give me eternal life today?

Christmas

Friday: The Living Christ: The Testimony of the Apostles   How does this strengthen my testimony of Christ?

Saturday: What things around me testify of Jesus Christ?

Sunday Reflection

Spiritual Promptings

Goal for Next Week

Dec 25-31

Monday — Revelations 15-16 What great and marvelous works of the Lord do I see in my life today?

Tuesday — Revelations 17 Am I on the Lord's side? Am I called, chosen, and faithful?

Wednesday — Revelations 18 When called am I ready to leave the things of the world and respond to the Lord's call?

Thursday — Revelations 19-20 How is the Millennium a blessing in my life and others?

Revelation 15-22

Friday — Revelations 21 What things can I do or overcome so that I can inherit all things?

Saturday — Revelations 22 Am I ready to see Christ's face or are there things I still want to do? What goals can I set for next year?

Sunday Reflection

Spiritual Promptings

Goal for Next Week

Thank you so much for your purchase! As an author and small publisher, I appreciate it. Make sure to check out my other books of interest at

joyfulsaintspress.com

I have a variety of study guides and journals for adults and children that can help you and your family enhance your Come Follow Me spiritual journey. I also have fun coloring books and word searches that align with the Come Follow Me scripture schedule.

Studying the Book of Mormon daily? Check out my Study Guide!

joyfulsaintspress.com

Check out the bonus coloring pages on the next few pages. Enjoy coloring!

ASK, AND IT SHALL BE GIVEN YOU; SEEK, AND YE SHALL FIND; KNOCK, AND IT SHALL BE OPENED UNTO YOU. MATTHEW 7:7

BE OF GOOD CHEER. ACTS 23:11

WANT MORE FREE COLORING PAGES?

Go to https://bit.ly/36hG5GL to sign up & download

Made in the USA
Las Vegas, NV
06 December 2022